Who's been writing this silly stuff in my diary??

First published in hardback in the UK by Scholastic, 2014
This edition published in 2023
1 London Bridge, London, SE1 9BG
Scholastic Ireland, 89E Lagan Road, Dublin Industrial Estate, Glasnevin, Dublin, D11 HP5F

SCHOLASTIC and associated logos are trademarks and/or
registered trademarks of Scholastic Inc.

Text and illustrations © Emer Stamp, 2014

The right of Emer Stamp to be identified
as the author and illustrator of this work has been asserted by her under
the Copyright, Designs and Patents Act 1988.

ISBN 978 0702 32503 8

A CIP catalogue record for this book is available from the British Library.

Printed by C&C in China
Paper made from wood grown in sustainable forests and other controlled sources.

1 3 5 7 9 10 8 6 4 2

www.scholastic.co.uk

THIS IS MY DIARY
(I is Pig)

You is **not** allowed
to be reading it!!!

(unless you is nice)

Hello.

Me I is Pig. I is 562 sunsets old. Well, I is guessing that is how old I is. I is not brilliant at counting. I got a bit confused around 487.

I lives in Pig House. Pig House is next to the New Shed. The New Shed is where **CHICKEN HOUSE** used to be, but the **CHICKENS** what lived in it was evil, so me and my best friend **Duck** sent them and their **HOUSE** up into space. If you don't believe me just ask **Duck**.

Duck is nearly always telling the truth. (And if he's not you can tell, 'cos his left foot starts tapping. I don't think he knows this happens, but I does! Ha! Ha!)

Pig House is opposite **cow shed**,
which isn't too far from **Duck Pond**.
I has drawn a map for you.

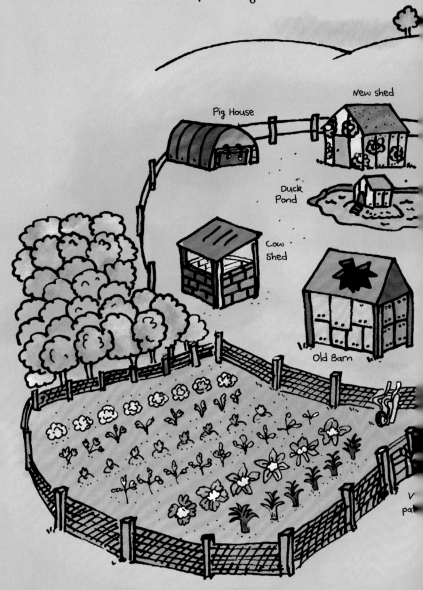

New Barn

Farmers'
House

Sheeps' Pond

I is called Pig. I has always been called Pig. It was the name what was given to me by the **Farmer** what used to

P I G

live here. I likes this name, so I has kept it. I thinks it suits me. But we didn't keep **Farmer** because he wanted to eat me, so me and **Duck** sent him into space too. I knows what you is thinking – this Pig is telling HUGE fibs. Well, I is betting you a big bowl of slops that it is true. And if you was knowing how much I is LOVING slops – yummy parsnips, delicious carrots, tasty potatoes – you would knows this must make it true. I loves slops sooooo much.

I also loves writing diaries. I is hoping my new diary will be very exciting so I is going to call it:

THE
Super Amazing
Diary of

PiG

Diaries is secret, but I has to be honest — this is not super top secret, because **Duck** and my new friend Kitty knows about it. But they doesn't know what I writes in it or where I keeps it.

I is also not knowing if it will be super amazing, because I can only write about things what has happened. Like what I has eaten, or what games I has been playing with **Duck**. Sometimes these is amazing, sometimes they is not.

But, anyways, here goes...

Boobleday

(As I is telling you, I lost count of the days so I makes up my own names. It's much more fun. You should try it.)

Hello.

If I is honest today has not been the most exciting, so I has decided that rather than tell you about unexciting things, I will tell you about all the things what has been happening in the days before I started writing this diary.

And, boy, oh boy, BIG things has been happening.

We has new **Farmers**! They is Vegytarian. This means they is not eating meat. This is very good only 'cos they is not wanting to eat me!

HOORAY!

But I has one problem; I is not sure what to call them. **Mr and Mrs Vegytarian Farmer** is very long to write and I thinks it will make my trotter ache. I thought about calling them MR AND MRS VEGGIE, but every time I writes the word "Veggie" my tummy gets all excited, and I starts dribbling and that makes my diary soggy. So I has decided to call them **Mr and Mrs Sandal** as they both wears these strange-looking things on their feet what **Duck** tells me is called sandals.

Mr and Mrs Sandal is super lovely.
They read the last diary what I wrote.
In it I asked for some **Vegytarian**
Farmers to come and take care of
us. And now, here they is! They is so nice
and kind. They gives me lots of nice back
rubs and **Mrs Sandal** makes the best slops
EVER. This is 'cos Vegytarians is REALLY
loving their veggies almost as much as me.
Yummy carrots, peas, parsnips, turnips,
cabbyages, potatoes – I gets them
all.

AMAZING!!!!

Not only does we have
brilliant new **Farmers**,
we also has a lovely white Kitty Cat. Her
name is Kitty. Kitty is very clever and

speaks lots of languages just like my best friend, **Duck**. She even speaks Pig, which is great because I can't speak Kitty Cat. I is not very good at speaking other languages. I can only speak a tiny bit of **COW** and I can understand a teensy bit of **Farmer** and **Duck**. When Kitty is speaking Pig it is sounding lovely. She purrs  her words. I thinks she could even say bad things and they would sound great. Not that she would ever say bad things, because she is SO NICE!

Kitty is the one what is giving me this new diary. She says that she read my last one too and loved it very much. I is feeling very good when she says this. Kitty is super clever, so if she likes my diary then this must make me a bit clever too.

I don't think that I could be any happier right now. Things has worked out sooooo well.

Bonzerday

Hello.

This morning I was woken up super early by the birds who has started sleeping in the tree behind Pig House. There is lots of them and they is singing VERY loudly. I is not minding their singing (sometimes I hums along with them), but I is wishing they would not be doing it so early.

Today **Mrs Sandal** gave me my breakfast. I is liking her very much. She has super-long hair. It comes all the way down to her bottom. All her clothes is very colourful and covered in these funny patterns. The one what I likes most is her dress what is covered in big yellow yummy-looking flowers. I has drawn a picture of **Mr and Mrs Sandal** so you can see what I means. I wishes I had clothes. I would be liking some with turnip patterns all over them.

When I eats **Mrs Sandal**'s slops I tells her how much I loves them. She always laughs,

even when I is not saying anything funny.

She calls me Piggybin. I has checked with **Duck** that this is not a bad name. My last **Farmer** gave me a name what I thought was nice, Roast Pig, but it turned out it wasn't nice, so now I always checks. **Duck** says Piggybin is not a good name and not a bad name. He says it means that I is like a big bucket what they pours all their leftovers into. I says this is a GREAT name! **Mr and Mrs Sandal** can pour as many leftovers into me as they likes. I is VERY happy to be a Piggybin. **Duck** says I is weird. I is not knowing what is weird about this so I says **Duck** is weird! Ha! Ha!

Being Vegytarian makes you very windy. When **Mrs Sandal** walks across the yard I often hears her bottom go *parp, parp, parp*. **Mrs Sandal** must not be minding about farts so I does the same when I walks across the yard. This makes **Mrs Sandal** laugh a lot. I is her funny Piggybin.

Straight after breakfast I headed over to **Duck Pond**. I loves hanging out with **Duck**. We is like two peas in a tasty pod, only he's a little bit cleverer than me and is smaller and covered in feathers. I think **Duck** would agree with this – well, all apart from the tasty pea part. **Duck** is not liking peas.

   We does everything together and

whatever we do, we has fun.

Today **Duck** counted while I had a competition with myself to see how many bubbles I could make in the pond with one fart. We is never getting bored of this game.

Then we watched **Mr and Mrs Sandal** in their veggie patch. It is huge; it takes up nearly half of **Sheep field**. They has put a special big fence around it and a big lock on its gate. This is to stop greedy animals like *rabbits* getting in and gobbling everything up. I has to say that when I looks at it, it makes my tummy go *rumble, rumble,* and my mouth go a bit dribbly.

I hopes they is growing some of these yummy veggies for me. But **Duck** tells me they is growing them to sell for money. He tells me that "sell" means to swap and "money" is this thing what **Farmers** REALLY like; it's little bits of paper and hard round things. I says these must be very tasty if they is happy to swaps delicious veggies for them. But **Duck** says they is not tasty at all. In fact you can't even eat them! Why would anyone be silly enough to make a swap like that?

While we was watching **Mr and Mrs Sandal,** Kitty came over. Kitty is a Vegytarian just like her owners. She says that she much prefers yummy peas and carrots to horrible-tasting MICES and rabbits. **Duck** tells me in secret that he is not believing her. He says he has never heard of a Cat what doesn't eat meat. He says that she is pretending to be Vegytarian to trick her owners into loving her even more.

I is understanding Kitty for not wanting to eat MICES or rabbits – not that I has tasted a MOUSE or a rabbit – but I is guessing that they would taste very furry. YUCK!

"Hello," says Kitty. "What arrre you doing, my loverrrly Piggy-wiggy?"

I likes it when Kitty calls me Piggy-wiggy. It sounds nice, especially the way she says it. I know **Duck** thinks it is a silly name though, because whenever she says it he pulls this face like he has just eaten something horrible.

"I is just seeing how many bubbles I can make with one fart," I says to Kitty, and I lets out a really big one to show her what I means. **Duck** counts eighteen bubbles! A NEW RECORD!!!

"Oh, Piggy-wiggy, that is wonderrrful," she says, and laughs a lot. "You arrre sooooo funny!!"

See? I told you Kitty was nice.

Chillyday

Hello.

Today was a very cold day. But the birds in the tree was still singing very loudly and waking me up. I is guessing bird feathers is stopping them feeling the cold like I do.

This morning **Mr Sandal** brought me my slops. Whilst I is eating them **Mr Sandal** sings this little song to me. I likes it very much. It goes:

TWEE

"Piggy, Piggy, Piggy, we love you,
Eat up your food, Piggy, and
make us lots of fertilizing poo."

I asks **Duck** what the words mean
and he says it's about how they
like to use my poo
to grow more
veggies. What
a great song!

When I went over to see **Duck** there
was ice on his **Pond**. **Duck** loves it when
there is ice on his **Pond** 'cos it means he
can slip and slide around on his bottom.
Duck is very good at sliding on
his bottom – he goes really
fast and does lots of
spins.

I wishes I could

slide around **Duck Pond** on my bottom, but **Duck** says that I is too heavy and the ice wouldn't be able to take my weight. He says it would break and I would fall straight through. That would be very bad because I can't swim. So I just sits on the side and watches, imagining in my head all the amazing spins and twirls I would do on the ice if I could.

When the sun starts to go down I is getting too cold to sit outside any more, so I headed back to Pig House to try and warm up. It is no fun being a Pig when it is cold. I don't have much hair to keep me warm, not like the **Sheeps** with their woolly fleeces or **Duck** and the birds with all their feathers. I wishes I was covered in nice warm wool or feathers. Or maybe both, that way I would be twice as warm!

I makes a Piggy nest out of my straw and I lies in it and does some big stinky farts to warm it up. Stinky farts is usually the ones what is the hottest. Do one where you sleeps and you will see what I means.

Just as I is doing this, Kitty comes over.

"Hmmmmm, Piggy-wiggy," she purrs.
"What is that loverrrly smell?"

I tells her how I is trying to get warm.

"Poorrr Piggy-wiggy," she
says. "I can
help keep you
warrrm; currrl
yourrrself up
arrround me."

So I does. Wowzers! It is amazing! Kitty
is warmer than all my stinky farts put
together. And she feels all soft and fluffy.
Farts never feel soft and fluffy.

"You is great," I tells Kitty.

"No, you arrre grrreat, Piggy-wiggy," she says.

Then she tells me the best thing ever.

She says that she thinks her owners is really liking me. She says this is the first time she has seen them really like another animal apart from her.

How good is that?!?! **Farmer** only liked me because he wanted to eat me, but **Mr and Mrs Sandal** really likes me and they doesn't want to eat me at all.

Kitty says they likes me so much because I loves vegytables just like they do. I is so happy when I hears this.

Kitty says she thinks it would be fun to have a "sleepover" tonight. She says this is where a friend stays at another friend's shed. I says, "YES, PLEASE." I likes having friends sleepover, especially when they is as warm and lovely as Kitty.

I is so excited. We is going to stay up late and play games. Kitty has invented this new one called "Who did that fart?". The answer is always me. We both finds this VERY funny and laughs A LOT. I hopes that **Duck** can't hear us 'cos I don't want him to feel left out.

I tells her she should sleep with her paws over her ears to block out the sound of the noisy birds in the morning. She says not to worry, she will have a special word with them and ask them to be a bit quieter.

Kitty is SO great.

Wongleday

Hello.

Kitty must have had her special word with the birds, because this morning they is not nearly so loud.

I wakes up in the best mood ever. I can't wait to have another Kitty sleepover. My tummy still hurts from all the laughing I did.

After my slops I goes over and tells **Duck** the good news. I is not wanting him to feel left out, so I fibs a little and says that Kitty told me that **Mr and Mrs Sandal** is really liking him too, but just not in quite the same way, what with **Duck** not being a Vegytarian like me. **Duck** eats **Worms**.

I used to eat them too, but I has decided to stop so I doesn't upset **Mr and Mrs Sandal**.

Duck says that I should watch out for Kitty. He says he smells a **RAT**. I says don't be so silly, Kitty is smelling only of Cat. **Duck** laughs. He says he doesn't mean Kitty really smells of **RAT**, he means that Kitty is dangerous. What a funny thing to say! He says some Cats can be very possessive of their owners and he thinks Kitty is one of them. I says I is not understanding what "possessive" means. He says that it means that Kitty is only liking **Mr and Mrs Sandal** to love her and NO ONE else. He says Kitty will not be happy that they is starting to REALLY like me. Not one little bit.

I says Kitty is not that kind of Cat. She isn't possessive at all. Kitty is wanting Mr and Mrs Sandal to like me. I is thinking that Duck is feeling a bit left out because of how well Kitty and I is getting on. It would be nice if we could all be friends. I decides I is going to try extra hard to make this happen.

Later on I sees Kitty sitting next to Mrs Sandal as she is milking COW. Mr and Mrs Sandal must be really liking COW'S milk, as they is milking her a lot. I wishes I could milk COW. I LOVES her milk sooooooo much.

"Hi, Kitty! Hi, **COW**!" I says.

COW can't speak Pig like Kitty can. She can only speak a tiny bit. I can't speak **COW**, so sometimes our conversations is a bit strange. I thinks that **COW** might be going a bit deaf, or have very big bits of wax in her ears, because she talks VERY loudly.

"**hi, pig,**" says **cow**, "**you look clod.**"

I think she means "**cold**". **COW** gets her letters muddled up sometimes. I whispers to her that I is wishing that I is having lovely long hair to keep me warm, but not to tell anyone I said that 'cos it makes me sound a bit sissy.

"**no worry, pig. woc no tell no**

one about pig wanting long hair!" she shouts back.

Hmmmm, I is making a reminder to myself not to tell **COW** any more secrets.

Mr and Mrs Sandal is giving Kitty a bit of **COW'S** milk in a bowl. I asks Kitty if I could possibly have a tiny bit. But she must not be hearing me, because she just drinks it all up without even looking at me.

"Oh, sorry, Piggy-wiggy," she says as she finishes. "I didn't see you therrre, of courrrse I would have let you have some milk. What a bad frrriend I am."

I tells her that she is a very good friend

and not to worry at all. Then I tells her that I thinks **Duck** is feeling a bit left out and how it might be good if we all spent more time together.

"Oooh, Piggy, you arrre sooo cleverrr, and **Duck** is so stupid ... I mean 'silly'. Of courrrse I will come to the stupi— I mean silly **Duck's Pond** tomorrow and we can all have fun, fun, fun."

Wooo-hoooo!

This is great news!!

I can't wait for us all to be friends.

Clonkerday

Hello.

I was so excited about the three of us all being friends that I woke up super early. Today the $birds$ was singing even quieter. Whatever Kitty said really worked.

After my slops I goes over to see **Duck**. I finds him wandering around looking for his little metal food bowl that he tells me has mysteriously disappeared. I says I wants him to make an effort with Kitty. But **Duck** says he has been watching her very carefully, and that I is wrong to trust her. Then he whispers that he has something important to tell me.

But just as he starts whispering, I hears

Kitty calling to me from across the yard.

"Come overrr herrre quickly, Piggy-wiggy. I have something exciting to show you!"

Exciting I thinks! Maybe it is a big pile of carrots or, better yet, turnips — my most favourite veggie EVER! I is sure whatever **Duck** wants to tell me can wait.

I runs off across the yard as fast as I can.

I hears **Duck** scream, "**No, Pig!**

NOOOOOOO!"

But it is too late.

For a moment all I can see is black.

Then all I can see is red.

I blinks a few times before I realizes what the red is. It's the big van what delivers these things called letters to **Mr and Mrs Sandal**.

I tries to stand up, but my legs feel all wobbly and my head feels spinny. So I stays lying down. Kitty and **Duck** rush over to me.

"Arrre you alive, Piggy-wiggy?" says Kitty.

"Yes," I says, "but my head feels very fuzzy."

"That is such a shame!" she says. "I mean about yourrr head being fuzzy, of courrrse. It would have been terrrible if you werrre dead."

Duck tells Kitty off for calling me across the yard when the red van was coming. I tells him not to be so daft. It was my fault for not looking. **Duck** says I should not be so gullible. I don't know what this means, but I is too cross with him for being rude to Kitty to ask.

Mr and Mrs Sandal comes out to check I

is OK and helps me back to Pig House. My head is still a bit sore, but it feels lots better after **Mrs Sandal** is giving me an extra-big bowl of slops. I is really not sure there is anything that could happen to me that slops could not make better.

Kitty comes in and curls up next to me. She tells me again how sorry she is. She says that **Duck** is wrong about her wanting to hurt me. She says she would never ever do such a horrible thing to her NEW BEST FRIEND.

Did you read that?!!!!

Kitty says I is her NEW BEST FRIEND. AMAZING!!!

Now I has two best friends. I is such a lucky Pig.

Kitty says that not only is I her NEW BEST

FRIEND, but that I is also her favourite ever
fart-maker. She says she has never smelled
farts as good as mine. She loves them so
much that she has brought these special
green plastic bottles with her to catch them

in so she can take them away and enjoy
sniffing them later. I says I is happy for her
to have as many farts as she likes. No one
has ever wanted to sniff my farts before,
not even **Duck**. Kitty must REALLY like me!

Fuggleday

Hello.

Today I has mostly been rolling in my special mud patch. The **Sheeps** all came over and watched. **Sheeps** is very funny. They is doing EVERYTHING together. I thinks that they would secretly like to roll around in mud too. But the mud would get all stuck in their wool and make them so heavy they wouldn't be able to move. Ha! Ha!

I then heads over to see **Duck**. I asks him what he was wanting to tell me before I got bonked on the head by the big red van. **Duck** says he has proof that Kitty is just pretending to be nice.

The other day he saw Kitty with one of the birds from the tree in her mouth. He says she ran into the Old Barn with it and when he went over, she was there, but the bird was gone.

I says I don't understand why this is bad.

"**Haven't you noticed that the** birds' **singing is getting quieter and quieter?**" he says. "**Who do you think is responsible for that?**"

TWEET!

"Well, Kitty, of course," I says. "She asked them not to be so noisy 'cos they was waking me up very early."

Then **Duck** says something really daft.

He says, "**She hasn't been talking to them, Pig – she's been eating them!**"

I tells him that is the most silly thing I has ever heard. Firstly Kitty is not eating meat, and secondly the tree is too tall for Kitty to climb.

Duck says I is not being able to see the wood for the trees. I is not really understanding why he is saying this. I can see the woods very clearly. They is not that far away from Pig House and the trees does not get in the way! **Duck** is saying some very strange things these days.

He says he won't give up. He is going to prove to me once and for all that Kitty is bad news. I says I is sure he won't be able to. We agrees to not agree and it is making us

both a bit cross. Instead we decides to play
this game where we has to see who can do
the most spins and still walk in a straight
line — **Duck** on the ice or me on the land.
This is very funny and we
both gets very dizzy and
falls over lots.

   When we has finished we
watches **Mr and Mrs Sandal** in their veggie
patch. **Mrs Sandal** pulls up a baby carrot
and has a good look at it. It looks soooo
yummy.

Kitty wanders over to see them. **Mrs Sandal** reaches down and gives it to her. Oh boy, I wishes I was Kitty. I LOVES carrots.

"**I bet she doesn't eat it**," says **Duck**.

I thinks maybe Kitty hears him, 'cos she looks at us, licks her lips, and takes a big bite out of it. She coughs a bit and her face goes all funny and scrunched up. For a moment I thinks she might be choking, but then she swallows and gives me and **Duck** a big smile.

"See, **Duck**?" I says. "You is wrong about Kitty!"

*

Just before bedtime I sees Kitty going into the Old Barn.

I has decided to tell her that she is my New Best Friend too (**Duck** can be my Old Best Friend, that way I can have two and it isn't a problem). I follows her into the Barn. I calls her name and when she turns around I sees that she has a **MOUSE** in her mouth.

When she sees me she drops it.

"Ah, Piggy-wiggy! I am so glad you arrre herrre. I found this poorrr **MOUSE** out in the yarrrd. He is not verrry well at all, so I brrrought him in herrre to see if I could make him betterrr. Do you think you can help me?"

I walks over and looks down at the

MOUSE. I is not sure what has happened to him, but he is not looking very well at all. He is not moving.

I tells Kitty that I doesn't know anything about making things better. When I is not feeling well I eats more slops. But I doesn't think that MICES is eating slops.

Kitty gently rubs the MOUSE with her paw. I sees a little tear run down her cheek.

"I think," she sobs, "the little MOUSE is dead."

"Please don't cry," I says to Kitty." I is sure you did the best you could."

I wishes I could give Kitty a big hug. But I is too big to hug Kitty. I would squish her.

Kitty tells me that she will dig a special hole for the MOUSE to lie in. She says this is what is called a "grrrave". She says that she wants to do this in private as she is embarrassed about crying. I says I totally understands. I doesn't like crying in front of my friends either. She tells me that this is the second animal what she has brought in here to save. The other day she managed to save a bird what had hurt its wing. She says she fixed it, and the bird flew away just before **Duck** turned up.

I knew **Duck** was wrong! Kitty is soooooo kind. I leaves her to take care of the poor MOUSE.

She really is the nicest Cat in the world. I wish I'd remembered to tell her she's my New Best Friend. I is sure that would have cheered her up.

Oddynight

Hello.

It is the middle of the night and something very strange has just happened. I is a little bit scared, but don't be telling anyone.

I was fast asleep when I was woken up by this strange buzzing noise behind Pig House.

I rolls over and takes a peek out of the little hole what is in the back wall. I looks up to see what is making the funny noise. The sky is super black, but I can just see this thing what looks like a huge bat flying around the tree; a bat with a very long tail. I is not liking bats, and this one is

REALLY scaring me. I has never seen one with a long tail or what is making such a funny noise.

I stops peeking through my peeky hole and I curls up in my bed and writes in my diary while I waits for it to fly away.

I thinks it has gone now - phew! I hopes it never comes back.

Freezyday

Hello.

I is very happy that there is lots of pages in this diary 'cos today I is having LOTS to be telling you.

Today when I woke up there was a super-cold wind blowing through Pig House. There used to be a long flat piece of wood tied across my gate what stopped this happening, but a few days ago it disappeared. I has looked around for it, but I is not finding it anywhere.

I is feeling too chilly to go out, and I is still a bit scared of the big bat what I saw. So after breakfast I makes myself a big Piggy nest and curls up and does some stinky warm farts and goes back to sleep. When I wakes up, Kitty is standing next to me.

I tells Kitty about the horrible bat. She says that I is just having a bad dream. She says there is no giant bats around. She would know 'cos she likes to go for long, peaceful walks at night.

Then she tells me something really exciting. She says that the pond in **Sheepfield** has totally frozen over and that we could go over there and do some sliding around on it.

I tells her that **Duck** says I is too heavy to go on the ice. Kitty says **Duck** is rude – that I is not too heavy.

"Piggy-wiggy, don't you trrrust yourrr cleverrr frrriend Kitty to know best?" she says.

"Of course I does," I says. Kitty is super smart, so if she says it's OK, it must be.

Wooo-hoo! I is VERY excited. I has always wanted to go sliding around on the ice. I wonder how many times I can spin around on my bottom?

Then I remembers to tell her that she is my New Best Friend. "That's wonderrrful, Piggy-wiggy," she says. "No one has everrr called me Best Friend. I am surrre we will be Best Frrriends forrr everrr."

I says we should invite **Duck** 'cos he loves sliding around too. Kitty says she already popped over and asked him, but he said he doesn't want to. She says she really wants us all to be good friends, but she is not sure **Duck** does. She says this makes her sad.

We heads off to the **Sheeps' pond**. I sees **Duck** on his own pond and waves. **Duck** sees Kitty and shakes his head. This makes me feel sad. Why is **Duck** being soooo silly? I is a little bit annoyed at **Duck** for not being nicer to Kitty. She is new, after all.

When we gets to the **Sheeps' pond** Kitty says she will test the ice for me. She is very brave. She takes a run up and slides across the pond. She uses her claws to dig into the ice and does lots of twirls and twists. She even does a somersault – AMAZING! She is even better at pond-sliding than **Duck** (but don't be telling him I said that).

She jumps up and down on the ice and says it will be fine for me.

Wooo-hooooo!!!!!
I takes a big run up and

Wheeeeeeeeeeeee!

I flies straight out into the middle of the ice. I spins around and around. It feels AMAZING!!! I is going to be the best Piggy pond-slider there has ever been.

But just as I is doing my third spin I hears an enormous **CRACK!** Then another **CRACK,** **CRACK,**

CRACK

and then *SPLOSH!*

I is not on top on the ice any more, I is in the freezing water underneath!

The ice has broken!! I can't swim!!!

"HELP!" I screams. "HELP!!!" The water is freezing and it is going up my snout and getting in my mouth. I can't breathe.

I sees Kitty staring down at me. She is super panicked and doesn't move.

All the **Sheeps** come running over.

When they sees me in the water they panics.
They starts shouting, but all I can hear is
the water going slosh-slosh in my ears.

Then **Duck** comes over.

Kitty doesn't look happy. **Duck** is waving
his wings at her, looking angry.

Duck slides over to the hole in the ice
and shouts, **"Waggle your trotters as hard as
you can. I will break the ice with my beak so
you can get to the side."**

I waggles and wiggles my legs as hard and as fast as I can. I manages to just keep my snout out of the water so I can breathe, but the water is soooooo cold it makes my legs ache. I is glad that I has not done any farts today. I thinks all the farty gas inside me is helping me float. I holds my bum very tight so no farts can sneak out.

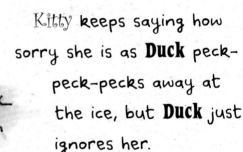

Kitty keeps saying how sorry she is as **Duck** peck-peck-pecks away at the ice, but **Duck** just ignores her.

Finally I makes it to the edge and pulls myself out. The **Sheeps** all gathers around me and warms me up with their woolliness. **Duck** is

VERY cross with Kitty. He says she was trying to drown me. Kitty starts crying. She says she would never do such a thing. She just wanted me to have fun. I feels very cold and shaky. I can't believe that Kitty would try and do something so terrible, but **Duck** seems sure. I tells them I just wants to be alone to think. I wobbles back to Pig House and lies down. The cold makes me feel very sleepy. I is struggling just to write this. I needs to go to

Blurbleday

Hello.

I slept like a Piggy rock. I didn't hear the birds singing! And best of all I didn't see the horrible big bat again!

When I woke up Kitty was curled up with me. She had snuck out some of her own veggies for me to say sorry. She is so nice making such a special effort to apologize. I would never give away my veggies, but that's how nice Kitty is. She says that she was just jealous of the fun what **Duck** and I had on his pond and wanted to show me that she could be fun too. She looks up at me with her huge eyes, and they is sooooo big, I knows she really means it.

She says she knows that **Duck** won't believe her, because he is not as clever as I is. Wow! No one has ever said I is cleverer than **Duck**. I is not sure I is, but Kitty is very smart, so maybe she knows something I doesn't.

I is not sure I wants to speak to **Duck** because he is only going to say nasty things about Kitty and I is not wanting to hear them.

I sees him in **Duck Pond** and I gives him a little wave. He gives a little wave back. In my heart I knows that I still really loves him, but I loves Kitty too. It makes my head feel very confused and my heart feel very heavy. Why can't **Duck** see how great Kitty is?

Womperday

Hello.

Has you ever had a jumbly day what is going really good, then really bad, then really good again? Well, I has. It was today.

It all started REALLY good with **Mr and Mrs Sandal** giving me my own Piggy jacket. They has made it out of an old corn sack. It is to stop me getting cold. Can you believe it? I HAS A PIECE OF CLOTHES!!!!

Now I is not only eating veggies like **Mr and Mrs Sandal,** I is also having clothes like them. Maybe I is slowly turning into a **Vegytarian Farmer – a Vegytarian-Piggy Farmer.** Ha! Ha! Ha!

I rushes over to show **Duck** but I can't find him, so I goes to the **Farmer House** and shows Kitty instead.

Normally I would not be going over to the **Farmer House** 'cos animals is not really allowed there (apart from Kitty). But today **Mr and Mrs Sandal** is going out on their special bicycle.

I knows it is special 'cos they built the New shed to keep it in. It has a big box on the front. **Mr Sandal** pedals and **Mrs Sandal** sits in the box.

I know, I thinks — I will surprise Kitty. Everyone likes it when their New Best Friend surprises them. So I sneaks up to the open window what looks into the kitchen where Kitty sleeps. I is just about to say, "Surprise! It's me! Look at my new coat!" when I sees three of the birds what sings in the tree behind Pig House. They is lying on the kitchen floor and not looking very well at all. Kitty opens her mouth like she is just

about to take a bite out of one.

I lets out a big gasp and she looks up at me.

"Oh, Piggy-wiggy," she says, "isn't it terrrible? I found these poorrr **birds** underrrneath the trrree behind your shed. They must have nearrrly frrrozen to death last night. I have brrrought them in herrre to warrrm them up. I was just huffing some warrrm brrreath on this poorrr one."

I is surprised the **birds** is getting so cold. Maybe feathers is not so warm after all. Poor **birdies**.

She taps one with her paw. It must be very cold, 'cos it has a little shiver.

"That's terrible," I says. "It's such a shame **Mr and Mrs Sandal** won't make them all special jackets like they has made me."

I does a twirl in the garden and shows Kitty the one I is wearing.

"Oh, how loverrrly," she says. "They have neverrr done anything that nice forrr me."

Her voice doesn't sound that happy. She must be sad they has never made her a coat, or maybe because she is so upset about the poor frozen birds. I wishes that I could make Kitty a coat to show her how much I likes her. I would make her the best Kitty-coat ever.

I offers to help Kitty warm the birds up, but she says she wants to do it herself.

She tells me to go off and have fun in my new coat. So I heads off to find **Duck** again.

I finds him over in his special bit of mud looking for worms. When I shows him my new coat, **Duck** looks worried.

"**Pig,**" he says in his most serious voice, "**this is not good. The more Mr and Mrs Sandal like you, the more jealous Kitty will be. Please be careful. She has already tried to drown you and have you run over. She is evil! I really think you should stop hanging around with her.**"

"**Duck,**" I says in MY most serious voice (I has never used my serious voice on **Duck** before), "you is VERY wrong. You is just jealous that I has another best friend. She is not evil. In fact she is in the kitchen right now, trying to save three birds from freezing to death!"

Then I does something else that I has never done before. I turns my back on **Duck** and walks back to my house.

I is so angry and upset it feels like my tummy is on fire. It is horrible. When **Mrs Sandal** brings me my supper I does another thing I has never

done before. I LEAVES MY SLOPS! I knows
you must be thinking I is mad, but I is just
feeling so angry and sad. I thinks **Mrs Sandal**
must understand something is wrong 'cos she
gives me an extra-long rub behind my ears.
When she leaves I closes my eyes and tries to
fall asleep.

When I wakes up it is night-time,
and lovely, warm Kitty is lying
next to me. My tummy
does a HUGE rumble.
Now I wishes that I
had eaten my supper.

  "Poorrr Piggy-wiggy,"
says Kitty. "You sound everrr so hungrrry.
Shall I tell you a secrrret?"

"Yes! Yes!" I says. I loves secrets.

"You know those delicious veggies that have been grrrowing in the veggie patch?" she says. "Well they arrre finally rrready."

"You mean ready to be sold for money?" I asks, feeling a little sad inside.

"No, silly," she says. "Rrready forrr you to eat!"

She tells me how **Mr and Mrs Sandal** has been growing them for me, their favourite pig. Did you read that? FAVOURITE PIG! First they pats me and sings to me, then they makes me a special jacket, and now they has grown me a huge pile of veggies. I is so happy my heart feels like it is going to pop out of my chest!

I knew **Duck** was wrong. No one would be

silly enough to swap yummy veggies for
yucky money.

"If you arrre rrreally hungrrry," says Kitty,
"I am sure they wouldn't mind if you had one
orrr two."

"Is you really sure they is ALL for me?" I
asks. I is thinking surely **Mr and Mrs Sandal**
loves their veggies too much to not have
some themselves.

"Yes Piggy-wiggy, they arrre all forrr you.
Mr and Mrs Sandal get theirrr veggies from
a place called the superrrmarrrket. Veggies
frrrom there arrre morrre superrr than ones
they can grrrow themselves."

What a great word "supermarket" is. It
sounds like an amazing place. I wonders
what super veggies is tasting like.

Kitty says that she will let me into the veggie patch. She calls it a "midnight feast". Amazing! She says she will get the key to the gate from the special hook where Mr Sandal keeps all his keys. It's just next to the chair she sleeps on in the kitchen.

My mouth starts watering A LOT. And my tummy gets VERY excited.

"YES! YES!" I says. "Let's go!"

I IS SO EXCITED I CAN HARDLY WRITE. I WILL TELL YOU ALL ABOUT IT TOMORROW!!!!!!

I LOVES KITTY SOOOOO MUCH!!!!! I THINKS MAYBE EVEN MORE THAN I LOVES VEGGIES!!!

I IS HAPPY!

HAPPY!!!

HAPPY!!!

Doombleday

Hello.

I is sad, SAD, SAD

I feels terrible. I is not quite sure what I has done, but I knows it is bad.

In the middle of the night Kitty comes back with the keys and lets me into the veggie patch. It is the most amazing place. There is rows and rows of all my favourite things. I doesn't know where to start. Of course I tells myself I will only have just one or two things. First of all I chooses a carrot. Oh, boy! It tastes sooooo good. So I has another one and another one and then I has a parsnip and some brussels sprouts

and some cauliflower and some broccoli. I
just can't stop myself. It's all too delicious.

And Kitty keeps telling me to eat more.
She is sure Mr and Mrs Sandal will be super
pleased when they sees how much I enjoyed
all the veggies they has grown for me.

I eats more and more and more until
I can hardly move. All the veggies in my
tummy make me suddenly feel very
sleepy. So I decides to have a little nap,

right there in the veggie patch. Kitty says this is fine too. She even fetches my jacket so I won't feel too cold.

But when I wakes up it is morning and I can't see Kitty anywhere. All I can see is **Duck's** face looking down at me.

"**PIG!!!!**" he says. "**WHAT. HAVE. YOU. DONE????**"

I stands up and looks around. Ooopsie! My naughty tummy must have got carried away. There isn't a single veggie left.

"**Quick, Pig!**" says **Duck** in a panic. "**You have to get out of here before Mr and Mrs Sandal see you.**"

"But it's OK, **Duck**," I says, "the veggies was all for me. Kitty says Mr and Mrs Sandal won't mind."

Just as I is saying this **Mr and Mrs Sandal** runs over.

I expects them to be a little bit surprised that I ate all my veggies up at once, but they is furious. **Mrs Sandal** is actually crying. And **Mr Sandal** is waving his arms around so much I worries they might fly off.

Mr Sandal says some angry words in **Farmer** and points towards Pig House. I wishes I spoke **Farmer** so I could ask him what I has done wrong. But I doesn't, so I just puts on my best sorry face and walks back to Pig House.

Duck follows me. He tells me he is super worried. He says this is part of Kitty's big plan to get rid of me. I says, "**Duck**, don't be so daft! Eating lots of veggies is only going to make me fat, not kill me. If that is Kitty's plan then it is the most rubbish plan I has ever heard."

I goes into my house and lies down. **Duck** lies down next to me. He says this is for my protection. He doesn't want Kitty trying anything else. **Duck** is so funny. I doesn't need protecting from Kitty.

I feels terrible. I loves **Mr and Mrs Sandal**. I doesn't want to upset them. I can't believe I has made **Mrs Sandal** cry.

Doomsday

Hello.

My head is feeling spinny today. First of all I is thinking that everything is going wrong, but now I is thinking that maybe it is all going right. I shall tell you all about it so you can see what I means.

When **Mrs Sandal** brings me my breakfast she looks sad. I tries to cheer her up by telling her I is sorry. She laughs a bit but then she starts to cry again. "**Oh, Piggybin,**" she keeps saying again and again. I feels terrible.

After breakfast Kitty comes over. She has this very worried look on her face.

"Thank goodness you arrre herrre," she says.

"Of course he is here," says **Duck** angrily. **"THIS IS WHERE HE LIVES."**

I gives **Duck** a look to tell him not to be rude.

Kitty tells me how sorry she is about what happened. She says there has been a HUGE misunderstanding. The veggies wasn't all for me. In fact none of them was.

"What a big surprise!" says **Duck**. He has this funny tone in his voice what makes me think that he is not really thinking that it is a big surprise at all.

"Exactly! A HUGE surrrprise," says Kitty. "I was so surrre that I hearrrd **Mr Sandal** say they were all forrr you, but I got it wrrrong:

they were grrrowing them to sell. I obviously don't underrrstand **Farmer** as well as you do, cleverrr **Duck**."

I so wishes I had believed **Duck** about the money.

"Oh, Kitty," I says, "I feels terrible. But it will be OK, won't it? I mean, can't they just grow more veggies? I will make as much piggy-poo fertilizer as I can so they grow super quick."

"Of courrrse it will be fine," says Kitty. "Therrre is just one teensy-weensy thing that's not so OK. **Mr and Mrs Sandal** arrre going to have to sell you to make up the money they have lost on all the vegetables you ate by mistake."

"SELL HIM?!?!" shouts **Duck**. "SELL HIM!?

"It's OK, **Duck**," I says, "I is sure Kitty has got it wrong. **Mr and Mrs Sandal** came here to save me. They would never sell me."

"Ah," says Kitty, biting one of her claws, "you see therrre has been a little misunderrrstanding therrre too. It was only me who rrread yourrr firrrst diarrry. I thought this place sounded so much nicerrr than wherrre we werrre living. So I cut out the map you drrrew, with my cleverrr sharrrp claws, and left it for my ownerrrs to find. It was all my idea. They have neverrr read yourrr diarrry. Oooopsie."

I starts to panic. This is NOT good. NOT good at all.

"I doesn't want to leave the **Farm**! All my friends is here!!" I says. I feels a big lump growing in my throat.

"Don't panic, Piggy-wiggy," says Kitty. Her voice is so calm and sweet – I told you she could make even bad things sound nice. "You'll all be sold togetherr. And to say sorry for all the mess I have got you into, I have made surrre you arrre ALL going somewherrre amazing - even better than herrre. Somewherrre with superrr-loverrrly new ownerrrs. It's the least I could do forrr my New Best Frrriend."

"How have you arranged anything?" says **Duck**. **"You're a Cat!"**

"Well," says Kitty, "I do have these." She flashes her claws and pulls out a piece of paper from behind her back. "I found this little adverrrt in the newspaperrr that lines my litterrr trrray. When I hearrrd what my naughty ownerrrs werrre going to do to you poorrr creaturrres, I cut it out and left it for them to find."

On the piece of paper is a picture of an enormous big **Farmer House** with a huge pond in front of it. Underneath it is some **Farmer** scribble.

Retirement home seeks unwanted livestock to pat and stroke.

Good prices paid for cow, sheep and pig

Call Horace on 07700 900332

Duck reads it out.

"You see?" says Kitty. "Thanks to me you arrre ALL going to this glorrrious place. The **Old Farmers** will pet and strrroke you frrrom dawn until dusk. I know how you and yourrr **Sheep** frrriends love your back-scrrratches. And, look, therrre is a loverrrly big pond for the wonderrrful **Duck** and a grrreat big garrrden full of yummy grrrass for your delicious — sorry, I mean delightful frrriend **COW**. I wish I could come with you, but my ownerrrs won't let me. Don't worrry though, I will come and visit wheneverrrr I can – and they will too."

She whispers to us that she has always dreamed of living there herself. She says it's the nicest place in the whole wide world. Nicer even than the **Farm**. But she doesn't want any birds or MICES to overhear her saying this. She wants this special place to be just for me and my *loverrrly* friends.

Wow! This place sounds even better than the **Farm**! Can you believe it?! And *Kitty* and *Mr and Mrs Sandal* can visit anytime. AMAZING! Suddenly I is feeling very excited.

I looks down at **Duck** to see if he is excited too, but he has disappeared. Maybe he has rushed back to **Duck Pond** to celebrate. I would, if I was a **Duck**, and was about to move to a HUGE pond all of my own.

Kitty tells me that *Mr and Mrs Sandal*

has arranged for **Mr Horace** to come and see how strokeable we all is. She says it is very important that we all lets him stroke us a lot. That way **Mr and Mrs Sandal** will get this money what they REALLY needs. I promises I will be as strokeable as possible. I doesn't want to make **Mrs Sandal** cry again!!!

Kitty helps me explain what is happening to the **Sheeps** and to **COW**, 'cos she knows I is no good at their languages. See, she really is very kind.

The **Sheeps** is super excited when they is hearing how many back scratches they is going to have. **Sheeps** LOVE back scratches (so would you if you was covered in wool all day long). **COW** tells me she was **"hungry"** to leave, but I thinks she means **"sad"**. Being hungry and being sad is the same thing in Pig.

I is sure that **COW** won't be feeling sad when she sees how much grass there is at the **Old Farmers' Home**.

I knows it is all going to be OK. Kitty would never be letting us down.

Enormo-Morning

Hello.

So much has happened this morning that I has to write it all down now so I doesn't forget anything later.

Mr Horace arrived just after breakfast. He is a very big **Farmer** – he may even be bigger than me!

He shakes hands with **Mr and Mrs Sandal** and they points over towards my shed. I decides to show them what a good Pig I can be. I wiggles my special jacket off and blows myself up as big as I can so I looks all squidgy and strokeable.

Mr Horace has very small eyes and his nose is very big.

He is looking like an **Owl** what has been filled up with lots of air. He doesn't seem to be able to stop licking his lips and is not smelling nice either. He smells a bit like inside the shed where my **Old Farmer** used to chip-chop his Pigs. I tries not to think about this.

His hands is very cold. They makes me shiver when he touches me. He pinches my tummy. This is not like any back scratch I has had before – it hurts a bit. Maybe this is a test to make sure I is not scared of being stroked a lot. He mutters a word what sounds like "**Bay-con**" as he pinches my bottom. I wishes **Duck** was here to tell me what it means. I is hoping it's a nice word.

I follows **Mr Horace** over to see the **Sheeps** and **COW** – just to make sure they is good too.

Mr Horace seems to like me 'cos he keeps looking at me and saying, "Dumb Pig". Dumb seems like a nice word – it sounds like "plum". I had a plum once. It was delicious.

When he is gone Kitty comes over and congratulates me and the **Sheeps** and **COW**. She says that we all did very well and that **Mr and Mrs Sandal** is very happy with us. I is so pleased when I is hearing this. At last I has done something right!!

She says that **Mr Horace** is going to come in his big van tomorrow and take us to our lovely new home. "I can't believe it," she says sadly. "Soon I will have to say bye-bye." A little tear runs down her cheek.

"Don't you mean 'PIE-PIE'?!!!" says **Duck**, waddling towards us. I has been wondering where he was.

"What rrrridiculousness arrre you talking about now, **Duck**?" says Kitty.

"This rrrridiculousness," says **Duck**, pulling out two pieces of paper from under his wing. **"This is the REAL advert for the Old Farmers' Home. It says,**

Retirement home seeks
unwanted pets to
pat and stroke.

Good prices paid for
kittens and puppies.

Call Felicity on 07700900716

"**woc no a puppy**," says **COW**, looking confused.

"**That's right**," says **Duck**, "**and what's worse, Mr Horace is no Felicity. Here is Mr Horace's advert.**" "**See what** Kitty **and her horrible claws have done! She stuck them both together!!!**"

On the advert for the Pie Factory there is a picture of an enormous black building with huge chimneys sticking out the top. It doesn't look like a nice place. Something about it makes my back go all tingly.

My head starts to whirl. "So **Mr Horace** was from the—"

Pie Factory seeks
unwanted livestock to
be made into pies.
Good prices paid for
cow, sheep and pig.

Call Horace on 01700 900332

"Pie Factory," interrupts Kitty. "That is rrright, you Dumb Pig!"

She has a look on her face what I has never seen before. She is smiling, but it is not a nice smile. It is an evil smile. The way she says 'dumb' makes me think it is not a nice word after all.

"Congrrratulations, **Detective Duck**! Yes, I have trrricked you all, and it's too late to do anything about it. Tomorrow you will be minced up and popped into delicious pies. I can't wait to trrry the porrrk and **Duck** one. Harrr! Harrr! Harrr!"

My stomach does a loop-the-loop and my heart is pounding so hard that it's all I

can hear. I feels like I might cry and be
sick all at once.

"But we is New Best Friends. New Best
Friends doesn't do this to each other," I
says, hoping that Kitty is just pretending
to be super evil.

"Oh, Piggy-wiggy, you stupid, smelly
crrreature. I can't believe you fell for that.
How it made me laugh when I rrread about
how much you liked me in your silly diarrry."

"You has read my diary?!!!!" I says.

"Yes, of courrrse. Why do you think I
gave it to you? So I could know just what
you werrre thinking. You thought I was
vegetarrrian. You thought I carrred for you.
You thought I didn't trrry to drrrown you or
have you rrrun overrr. You thought I made a

mistake letting you into the veggie patch."

Kitty grins even more. I is thinking that it is not possible for her mouth to go any wider.

"Tomorrow I will have my ownerrrs and this farrrm all to myself. Loverrrly!"

She turns around, flicks her tail in the air and walks off. **COW** is looking like she is about to cry and the **Sheeps** is all standing in a big circle, shaking. I can tell they is all very upset 'cos they won't look at me, even when I tells them how sorry I is.

Duck does nothing but slowly shake his head. I thinks he is about to tell

me how stupid I has been, but instead he
turns to me and says, **"Pig, my dear friend,
I think we may need an escape plan."**

See? I told you **Duck** is brilliant. How did I
ever think that Kitty was a better friend?
I feels so ashamed inside, but so happy at
the same time that I has such a great
friend. I wants to tell **Duck** all of this, but
I has this huge lump in my throat what is

stopping the words coming out. So I just
nods my head up and down. Yes, yes,
we does need an escape plan
and we needs one FAST!!
I will write in my
diary again when we has
worked out what our
plan will be.
I hopes it is good. I is
trying not to think about
the trouble we will be in if it
isn't. All the trouble I HAS MADE!!!

Enormo-Afternoon

Hello.

If you is thinking that this morning was unbelievable, just you waits until you reads what I has to tell you about this afternoon!!

First let me tell you how amazing **Duck** is, in case you doesn't know yet.

He says he still loves me even though I has been sillier than a Pig has ever been. This makes everything feel a teensy bit better, but only a teensy bit, because he won't be able to love me for much longer if we is both chip-chopped up and put in a pie!!!!

We needs to get **Duck**, **COW**, the **Sheeps** and me out of here before **Mr Horace** comes back.

Duck says we has to ask for help.

"Who is going to help us?" I says. "We only knows ourselves!"

Then **Duck** tells me a SUPER-UNBELIEVABLE thing.

When **Duck** was very little, his mum, **Mrs Duck**, told him about this elite (**Duck** tells me this means AMAZING-AMAZING!) squad of birds. She said, "**If you have a problem, if no one else can help, and if you can find them, you can hire ... the** Phantom Bantams."

I is imagining that they is these incredible birds with super-huge brains and amazing powers. HOW EXCITING!!

"But how is we going to let them know we is in trouble?" I asks.

Duck tells me that we has to use this top-secret special call. The problem is that it has to be VERY loud. The Phantom Bantams has to hear it wherever they is. It takes a whole flock of **Ducks** to do it. But 'cos **Fox** ate all the other **Ducks**, we is going to have to think of another way.

"I know," I says, "how about **COW**? She has a super-loud voice."

"Good thinking," says **Duck**. I always likes it when **Duck** says this.

We goes over to **COW**.

COW is still looking VERY upset. She keeps saying, **"no woc pie,"** over and

over, and she still won't look at me. **DUCK**
talks to her in **COW**. I hears him say the
words "Phantom Bantam", and then he
makes this odd crowing noise what goes,
"BOCK-A-BOOOODLE-WOOOOOOOO!" **COW**
looks nervous.

"**WOC CrOW?**"

We both nods.

She shyly has a go. I has never heard a

COW crow before. I tries hard not to laugh
'cos I know that would be rude
and probably make her
even more cross with me.

Duck shakes his head.
"Sorry, **COW**, it's just not loud
enough," he says.

COW puts her head down and
looks very sad.

"Don't worry," says Duck. "I've got an
idea." He drags her feed bucket over. "Kick
the bottom out of this, Pig."

I is a little confused, but does what he says.
He then helps **COW** slide it up over her nose.

"You is a genius!" I says to Duck. "It's a
COW-trumpet ... a crumpet!!!"

We all laughs, even **COW**. I is still funny,

even when things has all gone a bit wibbly-wobbly.

COW takes a very deep breath and goes, "**booooock-a-boooodle-WOOOOOOOOOO!!!!!!**"

Her voice is SUPER LOUD. It makes my ears shake. Even **COW** looks surprised.

We all stands in silence. Nothing is making a noise, not even the birds what is left in the tree. I listens for Kitty. I hopes she is having a very deep sleep.

I looks up in the sky, but all I sees is clouds. Perhaps not even **COW'S** crumpet was loud enough. Just as my heart is starting to sink in my tummy, I spots a dot of black in the sky. As it gets closer it looks more like the letter V. The letter V

made up of ... flying birds.

I is so excited I has to stop myself from jumping up and down. THE PHANTOM BANTAMS IS HERE TO SAVE US!!!

As they gets closer I sees that their wings is not really wings. They is wearing these large triangle-shaped things on their backs. **Duck** says these is called hang-gliders. He says Phantom Bantams is not being able to fly themselves, as they is a kind of small **CHICKEN**. But they is being able to make amazing things, like special glider-wings. Brilliant, I thinks. Maybe they will be able to build something to get us out of here. But just as they land I remembers he said the word

CHICKEN!!!!!!!!!

THE PHANTOM BANTAMS IS MINIATURE **EVIL CHICKENS**!!!

I is really not liking **CHICKENS** — they is VERY evil. The ones what used to live here stole **Duck's** food, pooed on **COW** and sent me off to Pluto in a space rocket what they built out of a tractor.

I looks at **Duck**. My face must look worried because he says, **"It's OK, Pig, they are not Evil Chickens. They are super-special** Bantams."

I is still really not sure about them.
They is very **CHICKEN**-looking to me. I
decides to test them to see if they sounds
like **EVIL CHICKENS**. "Hello," I says. The biggest
one steps forward. I steps back, just in
case he tries to do something evil. I lets
out a little scared fart.
It's a real stinker.

"Goeden day,
Piggenpoop! I ish de Ving
Commander of de Phantoom
Bantooms. Zeesh are my
shkwadren. Like your friend
de Quakenfloofer says, ve
ish not de **CHICKENSH**. ve ish de
Dutch Bantamsh. Ve ish from
de Nedderlands - a playsh far

away. Pleash be excushing the way ve ish shpeaking."

My stinky fart must have reached his nose, 'cos then he waves his wing in front of his beak and says, "Whoa, de big Piggenpoop is making de shtinkenminken guffenpuffs! Ja! Ja! Ja!"

They all laugh and wave their wings in front of their noses.

I feels a little better about them 'cos:

1. They is not sounding like EVIL CHICKENS.

2. They is laughing at my farts. The EVIL CHICKENS never laughed at my farts.

They takes off their hang-glider wings and folds them up.

"Shargeant," says the Ving Commander, pointing at one of the others, "bring out de pin and de pooper."

From under his wing the "shargeant" pulls out a piece of paper and a pen. The VING COMMANDER is not wrong about their speaking sounding funny.

"Now tell me, Piggenpoop, Quakenfloofer and Milkenmaker – vat ish de problem?"

Duck tells him all about what has happened and how we all needs to leave before **Mr Horace** comes back. The Bantam scribbles away. When **Duck** is finished, the Ving Commander says, "Wow! you guyshh ish really in de big poopen! But don't worry, ve vill make de mosht exshellent plan for you. Ve shall help you eshcape, no problem. **Mishter Horace** hash de van, so you vill need something fashter so he can't catch you. You need an amashing, aweshome rocket-powered eshcape vehicle."

All right! Now they is talking. In my head I imagines something even more amazing than the Trocket the **EVIL CHICKENS** built. A Mega-Trocket; the biggest and best rocket-powered vehicle there has ever been. It has rockets strapped all over it and it goes a million miles an hour. Wooo-hoooo! I is starting to really like the Phantom Bantams.

"All Ve need ish de materialsh to build it. So now Ve shneak around de farmen to find dem."

COW is too big to sneak, so me and **Duck** shows them around. I has to hand it to the Bantams, they is very good at

sneaking.
They tucks
in their wings and their
tails and their heads and makes themselves
very small. They looks like little balls of
feathers. They toddles very fast, still in a
V shape, around the yard.

we shows them everything and the SHARGEANT makes notes.

when we gets to the little shed where **Mr and Mrs Sandal** keeps their special bicycle, they gets really excited.

"Ve are loving de bicyclesh," the Ving Commander says. "Make de note on de pooper, shargeant. I think ve have found de eshchape vehicle, ve jusht need to make it go very farsht."

Yes, yes, I thinks — you needs to cover it with ENORMOUS rockets.

The sun starts to set. we doesn't have much time.

The Phantom Bantams tells me and **Duck** to make sure that "de Kittenkat" doesn't find them or see what they is up to. This is going to be hard 'cos night-time is when Kitty is coming out and creeping around. And now I knows why – she is looking for her dinner!

I has to go now and write more later, 'cos I can't do keeping watch for Kitty and writing a diary all at the same time.

Enormo-Night

Hello.

I is starting to feel that this might be the longest day what I has lived! Ever.

Not long after the Phantom Bantams started work, Kitty is coming out of the **house**. She sees us sitting on the edge of **Duck Pond** and starts walking towards us. Just as she does, a loud thumping noise comes from the small shed. Kitty's ears prick up.

Duck bangs his foot as hard as he can on the plastic bowl what he was given to replace the metal one. Every time there is a bang from the shed, **Duck** does it again.

"Sing as loud as you can," he whispers.

"But I can't," I says. "I is no good at singing."

"**Yes, you are,**" he says. "**Let's sing our favourite song one more time before we are turned into pies! Sing, Pig, sing!!**"

Our favourite song? Before we is turned into pies?? Has **Duck** has gone mad??? I checks his left foot. I can't tell if it is tapping or not, 'cos it is banging the bowl.

I is confused, but the way **Duck** looks at me says I HAS to sing. So I does. I sings the only song I knows:

"Piggy, Piggy, Piggy,
  we love you,
Eat up your food, Piggy, and
Make us lots of fertilizing poo."

Duck bangs his foot on the bowl in time to my song.

Kitty stops in her tracks and stares at us. The noise from the shed is getting louder. **Duck** bangs his foot harder.

"Amazing, Pig! What a voice!" he shouts. **"Let's sing it again!!"**

No one has ever said my singing is good. So I proudly sings it again, the loudest I can. I think **Duck** might be right, my voice is sounding great.

Kitty is clearly not liking it as much as **Duck** though. *"Arrrghhh, stop that terrible rrracket!!!"* she screams as she turns and runs off towards the woods.

As soon as she has disappeared into the trees, **Duck** stops.

"Phew! That was great," he says. "Cats **hate loud noise. Your terrible voice really hurt her sensitive ears – look how fast she ran away!"**

"But you said you liked my voice!" I says.

Duck just laughs. He is so rude sometimes!

Finally the banging finishes in the shed. The Ving Commander tells us to come over and look at what they has done.

I is very excited. I CAN'T WAIT TO SEE IT!!!

The Ving Commander proudly opens the door and beckons us in.

"Ta-dar!" he says, pointing at the bicycle.

My heart sinks into my trotters.

They has attached an old wheelbarrow on to the box on the front of the bicycle. They says there will be enough space to fit me, **Duck**, **COW** and all the **Sheeps** in. It still looks too small to me, but this is not the biggest problem. The biggest problem is that THERE IS NO MASSIVE ROCKETS! NOT ONE!!

I starts to panic. This is not a Mega-Trocket. It is MEGA RUBBISH! I is starting to think these Bantams is maybe not so phantom. Kitty may have fooled me, but I is not going to let anyone else do it. I looks over at **Duck** and does my best "They is mad" face. But **Duck** is not understanding it 'cos he says, **"What's up? Have you got tummy-ache?"**

"No," I says. "I is just wondering where the REALLY BIG ROCKET ENGINES IS???" I tries to say this calmly, but when the words come out they is quite big and angry.

The Ving Commander just laughs. "Don't be getting your knickers in a twisht, Piggenpoop! Dish ish a turbo-powered, shuper eco-friendly jet enchine. It vill make you go farshter dan a rayshing car, quicker dan a jet plane."

The Ving Commander proudly points at this tiny little box what they has strapped under the saddle.

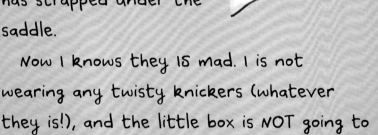

Now I knows they IS mad. I is not wearing any twisty knickers (whatever they is!), and the little box is NOT going to make us go faster than a racing car.

"Size ish not everything!" the Ving Commander says. "Trusht me. And the best thing ish that de engine is using de methane."

"Methane?" I says. "We has no methane." I doesn't know what methane is but I is pretty sure we doesn't have any.

"You hash lots of de methane," says the Ving Commander. "Ishh all in your windy bottoms. All yoush have to do is fartenpoop into dish funnel here," he says, pointing at a plastic funnel what is connected by a long plastic pipe to the teeny-tiny engine, "and *whoosh*, de fartenpoop will fly down dish tube and into de enchine, den, *zoooooom*, you vill be flying off down de road at a hundred milesh an hour."

Ja! Ja!

"A fart-powered bicycle... A Fartcycle!!!"
I says.

"Ja! Ja! Ja!" laughs the Ving
Commander.
"De Pigenpoop is making de funny joke!
Write it on De pooper, shargeant!"

I is glad that they is liking my joke, but I
is still not sure about what they has built.
I is not convinced that the little engine
is going to rocket us anywhere. I looks at
Duck, but he seems really happy.

I doesn't know what to do. I doesn't have
a better plan, in fact I has no plan at all. So
I has no choice but to pretend I is happy. I
puts on my best pretend-happy face.

The Phantom Bantams says they can
direct us to anywhere we want. This is

great, but we doesn't knows anywhere but the **Farm**. Then a MEGA-GOOD idea pops into my head. Why don't we really go to the **Old Farmers' Home**? They is looking for animals to pet and stroke, and we all loves being stroked. (Well, all of us apart from **Duck**. But in the picture there was a huge pond, and that would be great for him.)

Duck says he is not sure; the advert was looking for puppies and kittens. "Well," I says, "then they will be very happy when they sees us. We is much bigger than kittens and puppies; they will be having much more to stroke."

Duck laughs and says that I might have a point.

Yay!

I is crossing all my trotters that this plan is working.

The sun is starting to come up. I has no more time to write – we has to get out of here.

If there is nothing else on the next page then you is knowing that we never made it, that **Mr Horace** caught us and that we is now all baked in pies.

ZOOMZEEDAY

Hello.

Ha! Ha!

No, I is not!

That would be impossible.
I would never be able to fit me
and my diary in a pie.

Let me tells you what happened.

Before we could ride off on the Fartcycle we had to:

1. Squeeze all the **Sheeps** and **COW** into it.
2. Unlock the padlock on the front gate. (*Mr and Mrs Sandal* is always locking it at night).

I says that I will take care of number 2. I feels that as I is the one what got us into this pickle I should be the one what gets us out. I pretends to **Duck** and the Phantom Bantams that I is feeling all brave. But inside I is feeling like a big scaredy-pants.

I sneaks over to the **house** in the

same way the Phantom Bantams sneaks. I tiptoes very carefully on the very tips of my trotters and I tries to make my body as small as possible. Tiptoe, tiptoe, I go up to the front door. Kitty told me Mr and Mrs Sandal never locks it so she can go in and out.

She says she is not liking "Cat flaps"; they is making her fur messy.

I gives it a gentle push with my snout. Then I tiptoes in.

I has been in the **house** once before, after the last **Farmer** lived here, so I sort of knows where things is. As I pokes my head into the kitchen I sees Kitty fast asleep on a chair. Next to the chair is the keys to the padlock. They is hanging on the wall beside the key what Kitty used to let me into the veggie patch.

My heart is going *boom, boom*. Suddenly I steps on a little black feather. I remembers the poor birds what Kitty told me she was helping. I gets the cold tingly feeling along my back. I is thinking her belly looks very fat.

When I gets to the wall I realizes that I has forgotten to breathe.

I takes a huge, noisy breath.

Kitty's tail twitches.

I stands as still as a Pig statue but Kitty carries on doing her little Kitty snores – phew.

I has reached the key! I does a super, super quiet jump and I snatches it off the hook with my mouth.

I has done it! I has got the key!! I tiptoes as carefully as I can back towards the front door. I is feeling very pleased with myself. Then I notices a wooden box. I looks inside and sees TURNIPS. Mr and Mrs Sandal must have picked them before I ate the rest.

Oh boy, they looks soooooooooo tasty.
My tummy is telling my mouth to
have a teensy-weensy nibble.
If there was a competition
inside my mouth, turnips
would win the "Tastiest
Ever" Prize. And
Enormoday was enormous; I
    is feeling VERY hungry.
        I takes a bite. But now the
        turnip has a bit missing.
        It's OK though. If I eats the
    whole turnip, no one will know it had
a bit missing, because the whole turnip will
be missing. I really is clever sometimes.
    But before I knows it I has eaten all of
the turnips.

I feels very full. Worse than that I feels very windy! You know, the kind of wind you gets when you knows that there is no way you can keep it inside and that when it comes out it is going to be BIG.

PAAAAAAAAARRRRP!!!

I is right. It is possibly the stinkiest fart I has ever done.

"You stinky, stinky Piggy-wiggy!" a voice from behind me says. There is Kitty waving her paw in front of her nose. "What arrre you and yourrr vile bottom up to?"

I says nothing. I just runs as fast as I can out of the door. It's hard to run fast when your tummy is stuffed full of yummy turnips. As I run my bottom goes **parp, parp, parp**.

In the yard I sees the Fartcycle. **Duck** has done an amazing job of getting everyone in. **COW** is at the front with her legs hanging out. The **Sheeps** is all piled up behind her like a big ball of wool with faces and feets poking all over the place.

Kitty starts making a terrible howling noise. I knows what she is doing. She is waking up **Mr and Mrs Sandal**. We has to go before they comes out and stops us!

The Ving Commander grabs the key and runs towards the gate.

"Quickly, Piggenpoop! Git on de Fartcycle, you stinkenminken vindybag, and fly like zee vind! Follow ush. Vee vill show you viSh vay to go."

I climbs up on to the saddle of the Fartcycle. **Duck** is standing on the handlebars. He presses a button what starts the little engine. It is so quiet I can hardly hear it.

"OK, after three I want you to make the biggest fart you can," Duck says to **COW** and the **Sheeps**. "One ... two ... three!"

I sees the **Sheeps** all trying really hard. But **COW** just shakes her head.

"**me a lady,**" says **COW**, looking very embarrassed. "**lady no parp!**"

I hear the *pop, pop, pop* of little **Sheeps'** farts. The tiny engine makes a spluttering noise and the Fartcycle moves forward, very slowly.

I knew it! This teensy-weensy engine is not big enough to get us anywhere. I looks back at the **Farmer house** just as **Mr and Mrs Sandal** bursts out of the front door. They stops and stares at us. I thinks they is so surprised they is not knowing what to do.

Kitty is rolling around on the floor

laughing like this is the funniest thing she has ever seen.

The Phantom Bantams has got the gate open, but instead of us going OUT, **Mr Horace** is coming IN!!!!!

COW begins to shake. I thinks I sees a tear in her eye.

I feels terrible. This is all my fault. **Mr Horace** is going to turn all my friends into pies. I has to do something.

"**DUCK**," I shouts. "PASS ME THE FART FUNNEL."

Duck passes it back to me. I pushes it on my bottom and I concentrates super hard. (When you wants to do the biggest fart you has ever done in your whole life, you has to really concentrate.) I still has lots of wind in me from all the turnips I ate. (Turnips is not only winning the tasty competition, they is also winning the prize for making me the most windy!)

Mr Horace gets out of his van and

starts walking towards us. I can still hear Kitty laughing. I crosses my trotters that the little engine is as powerful as the Phantom Bantams says.

Then I lets fly the most ENORMOUS FART. The Fartcycle rears up on to its back wheel. The **Sheeps** and **COW** all falls

backwards. **Duck** has to grip on tight so he doesn't fall off the handlebars. Then *whooooooosh*, we rockets off across the yard and out of the gate.

The Ving Commander does this funny salute thing with his wing as we goes flying past. It all happens so fast, I doesn't even have a moment to wave goodbye to Mr and Mrs Sandal.

I is SUPER impressed. The Ving Commander was right after all. This engine may be small, but it is very powerful. I does my best to steer us in a straight line, but it is quite hard to steer when you has one trotter on the handlebars and one trotter on a fart funnel.

The Fartcycle goes left, right, left, right. I tries really hard not to crash into the big hedges what is on either side of us.

"**Uh-oh,**" cries **Duck**, pointing behind us. **"Here comes Mr Horace!"**

I looks over my shoulder. I sees **Mr Horace's** van. It's catching us up. We is fast, but his van must be very fast too. We needs more power, but I is all out. I passes the funnel to the biggest **Sheep** and shouts at him to fart his hardest.

Plop! I sees something land on **Horace's** windscreen. Up in the sky I sees the Phantom Bantams. They is taking it in turns to poo on his windscreen. They is very good shots.

Plop, plop, plop, goes their poos. Ha! Ha! Ha!

"**KEEP YOUR EYES ON THE ROAD, PIG!!**"
shouts **Duck**.

The **Sheeps** grabs lumps of grass
from the hedges as we goes along. This
seems to improve their farting. We speeds
up a little.

Behind us I can hear splat, splat, splat,
as the Phantom Bantams fills up **Mr
Horace's** windscreen with more and more
flying poo. It is almost totally covered!!
Mr Horace has put on these waggly stick
things to try and get it off, but Phantom
Bantam poo is too thick.

Hooray!!! We is getting away!!!

From behind I hears the Phantom
Bantams shout, "PIGGENPOOP! AT DE
NEKSHT JUNKSHON, TURN TO DE—"

Why has they stopped?

I looks up in the sky and suddenly gets a cold tingle. Something is flying among them. It's the scary giant bat from the other night!

"**a taaac!**" cries **COW**, "**a taaac!!**"

Silly **COW**, I thinks. We is not needing to attack. We is needing to ESCAPE. But then I looks up again and I sees what she sees.

A CAAAAT!! And not just any cat. It's Kitty!

On her head she is wearing a metal helmet what looks a lot like **Duck's** missing bowl. Across her back I sees a giant wing

153

what is made out of the missing bit of
wood from Pig House, and strapped to it is
the green bottles what she got me to fart
into. Except now they is upside down, with
fire coming out of them.

Kitty has built herself a Kitty jet pack and she is attacking the Phantom Bantams!!!

Worst of all, I thinks her plan is working. She swoops at them, trying to scratch them with her sharp claws. The Phantom Bantams stop pooing. **Mr Horace's** wiper things start to clear the poo blanket off his windscreen.

While I is looking at **Mr Horace's** car, I is forgetting to steer the fartcycle.

"Which way now?" shouts **Duck**.

The road ahead goes left AND right. I listens for instructions. But the Phantom Bantams is too busy being chased by Kitty to help.

I picks left.

We go *boing, boing, boing* down a bumpy road. At the end of it I sees a large black building. It's huge and on top of it there is two enormous chimneys.

I has picked VERY badly.

"OH, NO!" I cries, "THE PIE FACTORY!!!!!"

The **Sheeps** and
COW all starts to panic.
The yard of the Pie Factory is
very muddy. There is big boxes everywhere.

I tries not to crash into them, but the mud makes the steering go all wibbly-wobbly. We crashes into one big wooden box and carrots go flying everywhere. Then we hits another one full of potatoes. All these yummy vegytables and no time to stop and have a nibble!!

We hits a sticky patch of mud and the

Fartcycle suddenly stops. The **Sheeps** and **cow** is packed in so tight they hardly moves. **Duck** clings on with his feet, but I loses my balance and is thrown off the seat into the mud. I is not loving mud as much as normal.

Kitty whizzes across the sky and hovers over us.

"You rrridiculous animals," she laughs. "Did you rrreally think you could escape? I am going to make surrre you arrre all baked into delicious pies if it is the last thing I do. And who do you ALL have to blame for yourrr prrredicament? Yourrr useless frrriend, stinky Piggy-wiggy."

Kitty is right. I is the worst friend ever. I looks at **Duck**, **COW** and the **Sheeps**. Soon they will all be baked in a pie and it will be my fault. Tears start to fill up my eyes.

I hangs my head in shame and sees a potato next to me in the mud. Slops is usually making everything better, even the worst things. I opens my mouth and picks it up. Potatoes is so tasty.

"Harrr! Harrr!" laughs Kitty. "You arrre such a grrreedy Piggy-wiggy, even when you arrre about to be minced up, you still can't stop eating!"

Kitty is so horrible. I can't believe I thought she was my New Best Friend. She is my New Worst Enemy. I hates her more than the **EVIL CHICKENS** and **Farmer** mixed up together. I feels my blood getting hotter and hotter. I puffs out my cheeks and with all my mights I spits the potato at her.

The potato whizzes through the air and knocks one of the green bottles off her jet pack. For a moment nothing happens, but then Kitty is rocketing off to the left. She is not laughing any more.

She zigzags up into the sky. Her little legs is waggling all over the place. Then her jet pack makes a funny *putt-putt* noise and she falls down and plops into one of the tall black chimneys.

We all waits a second for Kitty to reappear, but she doesn't. All that pops out is a small puff of smoke.

Duck and the Phantom Bantams all lets out a loud cheer. Even the **Sheeps** and **COW** cheer, "**Well done, pig!**"

"Wow!" says **Duck**. "**I didn't know you were such a good shot.**"

"De Piggenpoop is shoow amassshing," says the Ving Commander, clapping his wings.

Wowzers! The Phantom Bantams and my best friend all says I is great. I goes from feeling very angry to very proud. I thinks maybe I won't be telling them I was really just planning to eat the potato.

I is just about to have a little victory roll in the mud when we hears angry shouting. I turns around to see **Mr Horace** running across the yard. In all my potato-blowing excitement, I had forgotten about him.

The Phantom Bantams take off in formation and I quickly climbs back on to the Fartcycle, but then I remembers we is stuck in mud and I is out of big farts.

I is pretty sure the **Sheeps** is out too. But then **COW** grabs the fart funnel.

"**no woc pie!!!!**" she shouts. I has never seen **COW** so angry. Her ears go backwards and her nostrils blow up really big. **Mr Horace** is so close to us I can smell his horrible smell. I hopes that **COW** is going to do something AMAZING.

And she does!!

She lets out the biggest fart I has ever heard. It's bigger than all the farts I has ever done, put together. I is having no idea that **COW** is soooooo windy.

The engine fires up and the wheels of the Fartcycle spin round super fast. Mud sprays out behind us. It covers **Mr Horace** all over, from his horrible fat head to his nasty fat toes.

"**ha! ha!**" shouts **COW**. "**eat that!**"

And then she does an even BIGGER fart that seems to go on

for ever and ever. We rockets across the yard so fast that
me and **Duck** is having to cling on so we doesn't fall off.

COW is my new hero. She is ACE!

The Phantom Bantams have to fly super fast to keep up with us. *Boing, boing, boing* — we bounces back up the bumpy path. Goodbye, Pie Factory, goodbye, **Mr Horace** and goodbye, evil Kitty!!

By the time we gets to the **Old Farmers' Home** we is all exhausted. **Duck** says that he thinks we need to be on **"top form"** when we meets the **Old Farmers**, so we all huddles up together and has a big sleep under a hedge.

It is fun sleeping in a big ball. It's all nice and warm.

Phew. This day has been looooooooooooooooo
ooooooooooooooooooooooooooooooooooooooooooooo
oooooooooooooooooooooooooooooooooooooooooong.
I can't write any more.
   Goodnight.

Oldieday

Hello.

I is going to let you in on a secret. This morning I is feeling nervous. The last **Farmer** what I knew was wanting to eat me. So I is a little bit worried that, even though they is old, these **Farmers** might be wanting to do the same!

We wakes up super early but the **Old Farmers** is already up. **Old Farmers** is obviously not needing much sleep.

Duck says we shouldn't leave the Fartcycle too near the **Old Farmers' Home**. We both agrees we wants **Mr and**

Mrs Sandal to find it — we is not thieves like Kitty — but **Duck** worries that if they finds it here, they might finds us, and then try to sell us all over again.

The Phantom Bantams says not to worry, they will push it down the road. We is on a bit of a hill, so it won't be too difficult.

We says goodbye to them as they rolls off. I feels bad for ever thinking that they is not great. I is wishing I could take back all the not-so-good words I wrote about them. If I could grow wings and feathers I would like to be just like them. I is betting I would make a good Phantom Pig.

The **Old Farmers' Home** looks just like it does in the picture. If I was a

Farmer I would be thinking this is a very nice place to live. In the garden there is a group of **Old Farmers** all sitting around a table. I thinks they doesn't have very good eyes because we gets very close to them before they even sees us.

They must be very surprised when they notices us 'cos a few of them lets out little farts. Ha! Ha! **Old Farmers** farts smells like old cabbyage! To be polite, I does a little fart too. Mine smells of yummy turnips. **Duck** gives me a look like I is being rude. But the **Old Farmers** seems to find my farting funny. They all laughs very loudly and when they does I sees the best thing ever: **Old Farmers** has no teeth!!!

If they has no teeth that means they can't eat us! PHEW!

We all spends the rest of the day being stroked and patted. Well, apart from **Duck** – he is exploring his new pond. Watching him swim around seems to make the **Old Farmers** very happy too.

I thinks I is going to like them a lot. I thinks they is liking us too.

Bimbleday

Hello.

Wowzers! The **Old Farmers** really is great. They is loving us all very much. I was right, we is much better to stroke than kittens and puppies. They lets the **Sheeps** and **COW** graze in their huge garden and **Duck** swims around all day on their big pond. There is an island in the middle of it where he can hide from **Fox**, so he is very happy.

They is stroking us ALL the time. The **Sheeps** is super happy 'cos there is this one old **Mrs Farmer** what likes to give them ENORMOUS back scratches. She then takes all the wool what falls out and

uses these stick things to
turn it into these funny
Farmer clothes. She has
also made me this special
Pig jumper to keep me
warm. This is great, because
I left behind the one what
Mr and Mrs Sandal made
me in Pig House at the **Old Farm**.

I loves my new jumper very much. It has
a big picture of my face on it.

The **Old Farmers** is also liking to
play games with us. **COW** is enjoying this
very much.

I is learning so
much about **COW** I
never knew. First I is

learning that she is VERY windy and now I is learning that she is really liking playing hide and seek.

At first I thinks it is quite hard for her. It's tricky to hide if you is black and white and very big. But the **Old Farmers** is not having very good eyes, so this is not seeming to be a problem.

So far they has found **COW** hiding:

1. Inside the shed where the **Old Farmers** keeps their outdoor chairs. (Well, some of her was inside. Her bottom and her tail was outside.)

2. Underneath the little bus what the **Old Farmers** go out in sometimes. I has no idea how she got under there. She must have really had to hold her breath.

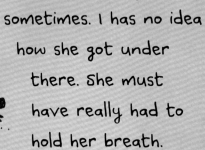

3. On top of the water fountain what the **Old Farmers** has on their lawn. I is thinking it must be made out of very strong stuff because **COW** is quite heavy.

But the best thing about the **Old Farmers** is that they feeds me lots and lots of yummy sloppy food. Turns out **Old Farmers** loves really mushy slops too. I guess this is because they is not having any teeth to be chewing with. Sometimes they is even giving me some of their **Old Farmer** biscuits. **Old Farmers** LOVES biscuits. They is always eating them and drinking this funny-looking brown stuff in a little bowl with a handle on.

One of them gave me a slurp of it, but I is not liking it at all.
It is yucky. But **Old Farmer** biscuits is YUMMY, YUMMY, YUMMY!

There is not much to do here apart from being stroked. When this is not happening I goes and sits on the edge of **Duck's** big pond and we plays our old games.

I is so glad that Kitty's plan didn't work and that we is both still here and not baked in a pie. I wishes most of all that I had never thought that Kitty was a better friend. No one could EVER be a better friend than **Duck**.

Upsydownsyday

Hello.

When I wakes up this morning my head feels a bit topsy-turvy. Almost all my heart feels happy, but a little tiny bit of it feels a bit sad. I can't stop thinking about the **Farm** and **Mr and Mrs Sandal.** I never wanted to leave them and I never got to say goodbye.

The **Old Farmers** has made me a bed out in the garage where they keeps their small bus. It is very comfy, but it is not quite the same as my old Pig House. I misses my special Piggy nest. I misses my

special mud patch – **Old Farmers' Homes** is not having mud patches.

I misses **Mr and Mrs Sandal**. They was so nice to me. I misses **Mrs Sandal** laughing at my Piggy noises, and I misses **Mr Sandal** singing me his funny Piggy song.

I goes and sits by **Duck's** big pond and tells him how I feels. He says he understands. He really likes his new pond, but he finds it a bit too big for just him.

He misses his old **Duck Pond**.

I says I wonders how the **Sheeps** and **COW** is feeling. **Duck** says he overheard the **Sheeps** saying they is starting to wish that **Old Mrs Farmer** wouldn't scratch them quite so much. A couple of them has big patches of wool missing and they is getting a bit chilly. He says he hasn't seen **COW**, so he is not sure how she feels.

It takes me ages, but I finally finds **COW** hiding up a tree. I has no idea how she got there. She doesn't look very comfortable.

"Is you turnip?" I ask. Turnip and

happiness is the same word in Pig.

"**woc broccoli,**" says **COW**.
Broccoli means "sort of OK".
Pigs like broccoli, but not as
much as turnips.

    I guess maybe **COW** misses the **Farm**
too.

    But there is nothing we can do. I is sure
Mr and Mrs Sandal is still believing that I
is a greedy fat Pig. I is sure they would
never have us back. I wishes they could
know that it was Kitty what was the bad
one all along.

Chewsday

Hello.

Today I is getting a VERY big shock. I sees Kitty!

Well, OK, not the real Kitty. A picture of Kitty, but that is still quite scary.

I gets up and walks around to the kitchen (I does this every morning to get my breakfast slops), and on my way I finds this picture of her. It's stuck to a tree. And underneath the picture of her horrible, smiling face there is some **Farmer** scribble.

I pulls it off the tree with my teeth. Looking at Kitty's face makes me remember too many bad things, so I tears off the bit with her picture on and gobbles it up. Ha! Ha!

Kitty, it turns out I was the one what ate you in the end!

I takes the bit what is left over to **Duck** to sees what the scribble says.

Duck tells me the piece of paper is something what is called a "Missing Cat poster".

He reads it to me. It says:

Lost Cat. Our lovely Kitty is missing. If you have seen her please emayle Hilary and Richard at farmers at veggielovers dot co dot UK.

I asks **Duck** who these Hilary and Richard is. **Duck** says these is the **Farmer** names of **Mr and Mrs Sandal**. Wow! What silly names **Farmers** is giving themselves. I much prefers the ones what I gave them. I is also not knowing what "emayle" is. **Duck** is telling me it is a bit tricky to understand. He says, **"It's what Farmers use to get letters delivered super fast."**

"I totally understands," I says. "Emayle is

a rocket-powered red van, like the one
what bonked me on the head."

Silly **Duck**, thinking that I is not as
smart as I is.

"Why doesn't we use the rocket-powered
emayle van to sends a letter to **Mr and
Mrs Sandal**?" I says. "We could tells them
what happened and explain that Kitty

tricked me. Then maybe they would forgive me and have us all back."

"**It's not quite that simple,**" says **Duck**. "**I am not sure Mr and Mrs Sandal are going to believe a letter written by a Pig.**" (This is a good point.) **Duck** says it would be better if someone else could write an emayle to **Mr and Mrs Sandal** telling them what happened.

"But who is going to do that?" I says. "Nobody knows what happened except us, **COW** and the **Sheeps**."

"**Nobody,**" says **Duck**, "**except anyone who might read your diary if you put it somewhere for them to find.**"

OK, I has to admit that **Duck** is much smarter than me. I bet he is as smart as you, maybe even smarter – but I can't tell because I is not knowing how big your brain is.

"But where is we going to put it?" I asks. I don't think that the **Old Farmers'** eyes is good enough to read, even if they could read Pig.

Duck says maybe, just maybe, we could ask the Phantom Bantams for one last favour...

Endyday

Hello.

This is the last time I is writing for a while. Yesterday we got **COW** to do the special Phantom Bantam call. This time we made a crumpet-trumpet out of part of the **Old Farmers**' lawnmower. It worked very well. Today they turned up.

Duck and me tells them all about my top-secret diary. Well, I guess it is not so top secret now 'cos **Duck** knows about it, the Phantom Bantams knows about it and now you knows about it. But I is sure you can still keep it a bit secret, right?

The Phantom Bantams says they knows just the place to drop my diary so that it can be found. I is guessing that if you is reading it then where they is thinking must be near you!!

If you is the one what finds it, I is really hoping:

1. You can read Pig.
2. That you is good at writing and is going to be able to use the rocket-powered emayle van to get your letter to **Mr and Mrs Sandal** fast.

Please tell them how I never meant to eat their veggies, how I is very, very sorry and how if they can ever forgive me, we would all love to come home.

I has copied the Missing Kitty poster, so

you can see where you needs to send the letter to. I has drawn back in the bits what I ate.

Lots of love,

Pig, **Duck,**

COW

and all the

Sheeps

XXXX